THIS REMOVED UTOPIA

Poems by Dennis Etzel, Jr.

Kansas City Spartan Press Missouri

Spartan Press
Kansas City, Missouri
spartanpresskc.com

Copyright (c) Dennis Etzel, Jr. 2017
First Edition 1 3 5 7 9 10 8 6 4 2
ISBN: 978-1-946642-22-6
LCC#: 2017948607

Design, edits and layout: Jason Ryberg
Author photo: Kevin Rabas
Cover art, *Tragic Prelude* by John Steuart Curry
All rights reserved. No part of this publication may be reproduced or transmitted in any form or by any means, electronic or mechanical, including photocopying, recording or by info retrieval system, without prior written permission from the author.

ACKNOWLEDGMENTS

Prospero's Books and Spartan Press would like to thank Jeanette Powers, j.d.tulloch, Jason Preu, M. Scott Douglass, Shawn Pavey, Shawn Saving, Jesse Kates, Jim Holroyd, Steven H.Bridgens, Thomas Mason, Beth Dille, Mason Wolf, The West Plaza Tomato Co. and The Robert J. Deuser Foundation For Libertarian Studies.

The author gratefully acknowledges the editors of the following publications in which versions of the following poems first appeared:

Microburst: "This last train should not be my climate," "You speak verbatim, television," "Yes, there is wheat, but," "Do I have to mention this Kansas," and "Sailboats drift through these streets, along with bullies"

Pirene's Fountain: "This forest sanctuary" and "From the highest point overlooking the city's wonder, apology"

Nice Cage: "We can reach out to the light" and "You want to stop being a man"

Please feel free to connect with the author at www.dennisetzeljr.com

CONTENTS

Envoi / 1
This Removed Utopia / 2
Pretend You Are Missing / 14
Dance With Me / 29
A Short History of Topeka / 38
To Photo the Future / 47

with deepest thanks to
Joe Harrington
&
CA Conrad
&
Amy King

Envoi

This last train should not be my climate
crisis, this spraycan palette my only prairie.
This last street can't be my boundary,
these buildings my only kin, the criss-cross
sidewalk a study in insomnia and my mother
coming out. What Catholic neighborhood vaudeville
drove us further inside? What circus was created?
When did the slurs first slide into that seventh-grade
language? I walk along where genius
was trumped by drunk fathers. *Everybody
who is a mathematician, into music,
peace makers,* she said, as in the historian
who explains the past as a vintage dress
washed and displayed for sale in the window.
We visit the tallgrass to forget what industry
does, what education funding Sam cuts.
This is captivation away from the cavity
left by his policies, walls from ruins.
Here, I clutch as an embryo, seeking a birth
in the sky's night transmissions. Here,
I am a constellation's diorama rounded
in fish-eye lens with bird's-eye view.

This Removed Utopia

This forest sanctuary
slides underfoot, spreads
and twirls vines and roots
against the darkness
with episodes of depression,
nausea, forgetfulness.
Sometimes someone asks
for a book of one hundred
most beloved poems, or for
a one-night stand, while
I realize I was meant
for building garden plots,
that I'm the kind that cruises
streets for not the road, but
the ruins, houses that housed
those who hated
my mothers, lesbians living
in the neighborhood, green
sprouting up to paint itself
an opera's last act, purple
hints spiking that Kansas City
Jazz, and whatever swing
I jumped out of landed me
in Roman coliseums, amusements
to dog walkers who chose

not to scoop up poop. Thanks,
I forgot all about that, as the hail
falls with cold rain, and if you
think me greedy or arrogant, I will
bake those black bean enchiladas
for the grandmothers inside you.

Just like the trees create mythology out
of old mythologies, you might guess
two mothers ask for the moon
twice, finish the yin yang
of Jungian dilemmas in which pillows
represent rest, insomnia.
I can tell the two apart, scene
from scenery, match from fire, but
what I mean is the rain
falls at some other time, since
the full moon is out and it is summer.
What else did you think branches
could represent, but every other
story your great grandmother wrote down
about milk, moths, and Topeka?
We can reach out to the light
over the tops, yes, that is the moon
without light pollution, and reach
the sea of tall grass, where our feet
live the rest of their days
rioting against electric walkways
the Patriarchy use to travel
on their way to the cattle slaughter.
I am ready to carry you
away from the execution line, yes,
this is real, no joke. Take hold of
my dark sleeve, my felt memory,
as we hope the dogs aren't let go.

You want to stop being a man, stop
those gym days and gladiator nights.
I am ready, too, for that bridge
I didn't construct well, but it's the only
way outta here. I didn't expect
to have lion muscles or the fatherhood
I learned from two women.
These lines are cast out wobbly
because they are ropes or words, you
pick. This is death's work and folly,
why we need that mythology.
How many times have I told my students
myth represents reality? Now we rely
on their belief, their faith, to hold up
our feet. Yes, I am just talking
to myself, as a woman with another woman
measures the patterns, holds up
yarn to the bulb, figuring
how the stitches will work
in this city.

I'm the novel the bookseller promised
would keep you up at night, the prodigal
son who worries about his mothers, not
the other son, the older one who inherits
regardless. If this is true, that this world
is revealed through online
encyclopedias, that my mythology is
of matriarchy and magical horses
leaving hoofprints on my forehead,
then it's cruel for these Sam
flash mobs of flame holders
to come to drive everyone
not him out, like sung
in old reveries.

And of course there is laughter, our thunderous
serenades to park creatures who remained
fearless in remaining, our picnics
at three in the morning, bellies full
of chuckling, your aimless run
into night's melody, my fatherhood
watching my children twenty years
from now, insisting that rain
revisit us in her odes. Ghosts of the matriarchs
turn outlaw, revisit and dare us
to look up again at their starry remains.
Grandma Ruby, the Royals are doing better
again, but my bones bare themselves
on my sofa, regardless of your occupation
with filing away forms or my dedication
to words. What happened
to your old sofa, the color of blue
oceans envy, that blackbirds aim
to replicate under sun? You stand
singing summer again, take me out
to the field of your hair, throw one last
pitch that pops popcorn.

What you call a weed is wonder, a caution
to enter the seat of my mind, all things
grown like vine, each leg of the river
becomes a park designed with in vitro
plans. Curves the streets make
surround like lovers. What I mean is:
there is sweating, a heart beats
out morse code with no tenure
for trees. I get hired as a professor
planner kind of milieu, as my
University tells me these greens
won't be here that long. Let's replan
what people see as they drive
by, old fashioned avenues
to grab attention with cutting edges,
needles to skin.

This removed utopia
robins flock away from
having sex. Multiply,
because, *devoting yourself
to a woman and having a child
will not make your life less important,*
says he, Shakespeare. That's what this
is about? Some kind of argument over
property, desire, and nothing
made of glass? Elf you, stomach
Patriarchy! You know a fish can make
itself a room shaped without lines.
This grass cemetery houses those
sea critters of ol' alongside civil war cannons,
as even the monks are men who crave
gunfire, so how can I find the peace
anymore, Osiris? You are going to tell me
right on my lips that Cyrus was right,
that Ed is, when he tells me I should
get the elf out of this town
as its sludge creeps, as one
doesn't know he is already in the hospital?

Every now and then now
feels like the last now
I felt just a moment
before, and I know this
town like the back
of my lair, this landscape
easily fits here or
everywhere. I can fabric
myself into this
as a mythology, which means
reality, or be that fiction
you coastal people call
Ozian-dreamer. There is
horizon, so there is sun
I am gaining each day, each
night a yard to move around in
removing the city at whim.

This is dangerous, which means no solace, no energy
to be alone in. These cicadas again, yes, even as poets
elfing have to put them in any Kansas poem, are real
annoying, clawing up my jeans as I hope
my fetal position outrubs their leg-song, some
kind of begging for the mercy licking can aid in.
Acoustics blaze, and these little deaths,
yes, I mean orgasms, dare I say in Topeka, could bring
everyone to morning, to being caught in a two-way.
My hands itch from the grass and rising dew,
so read whatever bursts you want into this. I've held
squirrels, possums, and nature does not end there
as gold is found in them trees, accents
of nature's curves, but I don't mean land-as-woman,
you post-colonial walls! Her breath in my eardrum
makes me feel naked green, sunflowery in spitting
seeds, makes me know how much I want
out of breath, stars, and constant horses coming
out of the sky. There is too much at risk here,
though. Valkyries of my mothers watch guard
in holding patterns, but are under attack, too,
if you count dubbed voiceovers, people speaking
for us, so they say, from the State Capitol. The need
for pharmaceuticals created blockers, marginalized
with pseudo-frames associated with everything
here, outside.

It's about the time I said things in smoke, nothing
from my mouth or chin to help suffering or ease
the nothing that places cars in reverse. This town's
selfishness feels its blind language between two people
acting like friends. I have a way through my body
of knowing, call it a gut cough, the boots
from the railroad workers passed down through
steel bars and barstools, one could always spend
their retirement on another beer felt in the kidneys.
Where was there ever a ballerina in this endless
hammering? Yes, this is another elegy
I end up writing for you. This you could be anyone
in satire, as this is, by the way, Topeka, by way of Kaw,
AT & SF, LGBT, and hate, so how does that feel?
Instead, let me take this crux of spinning along
with that beer to pour into poetry, take the rubbing
of two lovers, birds that announce the morning
with their site fidelity, lakes and parks rising
simultaneously, my hair and your news without
any chatter from televisions, secret politics
which align in favor of us all.

I carry one bird, two moons,
and three mothers, the two
I was raised by and the one
I married while climbing
out of this swamp of malls,
investments, corporate days
of cubicle nests no bird touches.
This continent of Topeka
doesn't overshadow the town
we remain in, whose park's
blackberries multiply. We take in
the cardinals and wrens, the injured
children who seek that home
they know as home but discover
for the first time, beginning again
is what love embanks, until we
get to the tiniest we we can be.

Pretend You Are Missing

Vampires live, not undead, but in genius,
in unchecked lines cutting through circles
of bone and soul, these connections imagined.
Please let my boys grow without this field, without
having backpacks, snacks, comic books, and friends
taken away. I'm not able to claim the track
or the martyrdom. My trials are snowbound.
My races turned to shaking my fists at buildings, cars,
insects, and dungeons that existed
only to me. My class thirty-eight fighter
lasted years of play, alone, no one to challenge
him, fists from the page. Fists formed in swamps
from miles away in other states.
Now that I walk this town to welcome ghosts,
my demise is somewhere in one of the faces
I had, recreated four times I'm aware of, except
for the boy that mows the yard every week,
or daydreams about The Watcher keeping track,
never interfering. Just join me as we call on
the moon to bring us out
of its broken face, to raise us.

These posters from the 1980's
keeps this place in the 1980's.
How would I know I would miss
the Meat and Cheese Shoppe,
circa 1985? Ballet Troupe, 1984.
Do you mind if I wear this poem
upon my head? Georgia O'Keeffe,
New Mexico Museum of Art,
1983. There are no children here.
Breakfast of Tiffany's staring
inside the glass while holding
take out, a paper bag and cup.
You have a good day yourself.
Do you mind if nostalgia pins
rock band buttons through
your heart? So what if you can
dim your table light yourself?
Sentimentality stops the missile
launch, stops the missiles from
launching, stops Ronald Reagan's
index finger.

I hope your deep-end memory
finds gold at the bottom, that the moon
shines wide across your surface.
I admit, I was a cook in search of kitchens,
worried about what dawn would bring.
In my young age, I learned to kick
those who would drag me down
underwater, hysteria an answer
made with fists. I hope my fishing line
doesn't snag the bad genetics
for my boys. What were you doing
again, waiting for the day
to shut down? I hope this landscape
doesn't crash in for you as it did me
when redemption was a foreign word.
The ocean makes contact
from far away over the wires
we hung up, together, and I hope
I didn't hurt you when you were that clown
pulling me underneath. If you want to know,
sadness is often symmetrical. The song
a heart sings gets curled with sweet
roses close by. I don't mean
any of that Romantic Era construction,
but real weight. I miss what my DNA
kept down, a layer of film on the water
fingers broke as they dove into the pool.
Still, I try my best to swim echoes to you.

I steer my summertime to the library's side
hoping no one sees my stuffed backpack.
No wings here, nor cape, nor antennae.
I am another form of life, sympathetic,
cracked. I'm fourteen, of course,
as my film's soundtrack follows me
in its buzz of bees. Someone could tell I needed
so they let me in. You think I am alien,
but isn't it everyone who follows along
this world of giants? Some other country
always in another direction serves a threat,
so the language says. Someone get Russia
on the phone, before mister President
picks up his. Come in, Canada. Come in,
France. Come in, unconscious tourists.
Come in, Martians. Come in, Issac Asimov.
Someone is out to eat the earth, eat the ocean.
Someone is belly-up enough to get orchestras
to play swan songs of nuclear flames.

Pretend you are missing, but go
to your desk anyway, a pupil
with an eye for absence.
Stare into the blackness of the board
until language appears
in your hands, caught. Hide
away your treasure. Salt
your wounds, water the land-buried
flowers. Write down the names
of monsters in the dungeon, types
of dragons, different cloaks
for invisibility and protection.
Say aloud, *Here there be traps,*
as they spring up or drop bottom.
Put into proportion many things
inside the bag of holding.

Throwing up faux peace signs, I make my way
to what writing does to vanquish my monster
depression junkie. I am hooked, then color
hooks me onto its backyard, a green of protection.
Justice is the window one can jump out
into a rocket. Spring doesn't have to be a weapon.
Instead, make the ego play a sparrow. Make
the mockingbird eat crackers until it's right.
Take down the Wolverine figurine to make space
for your feet, taking down the noose and your
reflection as neither help make moon or waves.
Take supper down to the pond, down to the pen.

Dial tones reach out here now, as well as beauty
in counterfeit speaking. Take your pulse, pioneer,
in the undiscovered discovered. Yes, wheat fields
were here up to the Nineteen-Eighties, growing
battleships heading to Russia. Honey stuck
on the boots, it's easy to suck the milk out
of lavender, to cry at the turn of a book
found in small-town stores with moose-head walls.
My ribs ache. My heart forms a bodice, my hug
wears a dress. I am a foreign soldier
in the way I grow my beard, whispering
hello out of hesitation, worry. With your soft
good morning, I know we can get out of here.
We can hammer a path for nature's hands.

Stars explode again. With kind of a government rule,
police do not protect, and that feeling in my stomach
grows fingers, bisects the lanes. Parasites
tailgate, even the ones who are on call.
There is another universe every time someone
crosses, as each traveler renames the things
seen, what they serve, in which order.
Then she or he remembers the centipede
following closely, inches away, only windshield,
blue and red lights on top seen
in the rear view mirror.

What kind of pencil drives someone
to anger? What kind of puppet gnaws on
other puppets, moths set free in the brain?
We become gypsies if we are to live again
in treetops, within roots. Even the butterfly
is saved, uncut, if we are to hermit surrounded
by crows waiting to peck, getting off on our worry.
Why are there flames in the windows?
Why do the stones carry hours? Why are fish floating
in rivers? This reluctant green goes unseen
tonight. This corrupt fight begins with isolating us
lonely carp and catfish, alone in passing.
I'm the kind who hides in summer
beneath moth wings and milky way
as myth dissolves on my palate.
These towns shadow this city
of shabby white, terra cotta death
as Sam brings his Roman ruin.
Sheets of ice raise to the surface, their hearts
reduced to locks. People love things
inside their homes, so why tremble?

You speak verbatim, television,
in the prompter's symmetry. I read
this book already, so have it, friend.
The prefix is lackluster jungle gym
with bars to swing back and forth, dropping
into mystery. Still, their gruntwork
will make Kansas what it was, coral
shelf exposed. We will divide,
anti-Kansas, pro-slavery
in the ways ships embed the prairie.

Even the beer packs a sparkle of talk, takes down
bathroom stall doors. If my exotic afternoon speaks
this fast, what should I expect from night's rising
grass and bar stools? He's a mean puppy, tail
wagging in the motion of weeds in wind. He says,
I will slay you, that god of indifference. His stomach
vines alcohol upward and Topeka's voodoo
does its trick again, anywhere I rest my elbows
in friendly rejection. I can now see the hops poured
within Kansas wheat, his nectar. Can we talk
anymore, brush by each other flannel touching flannel?
If this were a film theory class, we could be in love
man-to-man, stare-to-stare, showdown-to-showdown.
But I am afraid. Masculinity stirs a draft glass
swirling the moon, and we'll come to blows
in the blaze of burning fields.

Yes, there is wheat, but
there is John Brown, too,
if you want to have a mastery
of vengeance. I thought of a swamp
in my cup, countries of origin,
centers of conflict, and, exactly!
Yeah! That's why we stopped
doing it in competitions. An extract
of nature leading to silence, as
every table wants its pages, every
servant put to work. Fellas
from Missoura sneakin over,
I could not figure out the science
of it, the thought behind action,
what the stop point could be, if
there is one, and, oh,
yeah, people never ask how it feels
in the beginning.

This place just off the freeway, the city's
mouth, halfway on a drive from Oklahoma
to South Dakota, while I'm its traveler
with a traveler's look on me and need
black coffee in a white cup the white
of Sacre-Coeur. A tall macchiato
seems upside-down, but it is upside-down
in Seattle, too. My coffee tastes
my dreams, my eyes. I took the night
shift and the sun would always come up
in Wyoming. They even spell my name
right here, the little things, as my boss
looks for me somewhere else, my
landlord has no idea the *they*
he refers to is me and my kin. We are
the height of the moon, the lives
that burn at birth and death. I take
a peak at the veins through the reclaimed
urban wood table, those mythologies that run
along the backs of Colorado's mountains, through
the rivers of the Midwest—mine, yours, and
the person in the cozy chair we greet.

In the waterfall, the water demands
falling, the mind's scattered
tornadoes that carried my fairy worlds
away. Yes, this is Kansas and I am under
here a grave. Well, I'm not
dead, but some guitar player in me
has no guitar. These fireworks fade,
so snap a picture, move it to Instagram
to create a faded look. Along these bushes
are the Santa Fe Trail which almost
did me in with its natural atmosphere.

Do I have to mention this Kansas
again? Just there, people are learning. Things just got
curious, as the railroad is moving in us. Yes,
you're here. We use the observatory, too, zoom
in on the fires at night. Those buried stars under
the grass ask for spring, when autumn misses us already.
Did you want me to read your elegy now?
I drink cabernet to our high jinx back in the day, sip
to the convenience of Redbox. Wasn't it just over there
that Damascus was formed, then abandoned us?
Wasn't it those faint tower bells that brought us
back to the ground?

Dance With Me

Eve, and don't forget
Lilith. Women symbolic
as trees, as men
come to shoot
fire arrows. They
are still in pursuit
then? I mean,
men? I hate
Joseph Campbell
and his lackeys.
I'm getting off point.
Still, a village is without men
because of raids, approached
via a mournful soundtrack.
The women scarred to protect
their children from evil.
This fairy tale dagger
I refuse like masculinity.
I need to get away
from the castle. I can afford
the dark forest.

We've got restaurants, violin players! This property
still going fast, stay on my right wing. Make a play,
gang. This private chain goes public, just follow
where the fossils are dumped out. Tuna wish
not to be here, alongside spiral-shaped gastropods
for sale. We just want your pink. Look at America,
ain't she a beaut? Maize for everybody, look at cows
caged with chickens, they get along. Get you
confectionary fix on either shore of Wanamaker Road,
muddied by domestic grazing. Land! A house in the
country on top of that hill overlooking Topeka.
Two-bedroom, post-lesbian marriage in hiding,
off the Kansas grid. The water department reports
to the newspaper, scandal. This zoning is for man-
and-wife, embroidered legals who are of meat-eating
United States blood. This railroad still tracks through
here, pennies flattened due to the recession.
Can you feel the peripheral smoothness caused by
heteronormative clutter? My body is stiff, sleepy.
I want to tear my seams sown by pamphlets
shared in elementary schools. Those history books
burned donated photographs, souls taken.
Women-couples died in their marching dresses
shot like rabbits.

Only closed homes circle the block with privacy fences,
signs warning no trespasses, as we forgive those
Fred Phelps followers day after day, now
as he embraces dust to dusts in an open field
somewhere without a funeral. How many gray
mornings brought a coat, top hat, and gloves
to tapdance a vision of markers, this Topeka
going down in a hole? Movie critics give it
two middle fingers up. I haven't. It's tough
to swim this city who hated my lesbian mothers
all those decades, some still in the lagoon
sending bills through. The railroad leaves its metal
taste, every dancing incomplete, but we keep
the Jazz on, or whatever music one
appreciates in awakening. I mean the chlorophyll
pulled away from the eyes. See how people
love each other, grew up with family values,
even mothers, mine, go to church, share
a bed, and death does not them part.

Sailboats drift through these streets, along with bullies
on bikes with playing cards clipped to spokes,
all the ghosts resurrected through others. It can feel
foreign being a girl and lesbian, like a random seizure
one can't stop. If that lovely cross returns as a material
possession, it must be from the religious straight-jacket
blindspot. Squint for the people walking to church,
dollar-designated solemn submission. Kings open
their wallets to rid themselves of enemies, so they pick
you, so you hide. Farmers set blazes to burn their fields,
done on purpose. What grows can't be stopped, though,
a sacrifice for the palace, a cake for surviving McCarthy,
Homeland Security, Sam. This eagle will come out
phoenix-style, a woman, pushing their sums back
to burn their false-shroud-of-Turin flags.

She provided amenities, tea, chairs
to get the words down and out, accoutrements
for the oncoming battle. It turns my gut
to think Seattle, Boston, Los Angeles, and Des Moines
rank as *top places to go right now,* while
Topeka fights to uphold omission, undone plans
made in nightly promises. Yep, that's why
they go up ta Iowa, then come back for the reception.
One breath and I'm held in incantations, indentations
of mid-step, more hello than congratulations.

Espresso and wine holds me in surface futures,
Jesus looking down held in atrophy. I mean,
my two mothers are Christians, for God's sake,
accepting any Salamun or Shalom as well.
What is a sad place but an unprotected site
with painted mural to represent what could be?
Our Women of Sorrow, gestures made, secret dancing
behind America, some *man's wife*, Amy says,
married down. Rings molded for a reason, can't we
segue into inevitable truths, freedoms now drained
we can refill now? Hey, you, man! Should I clarify
that man in office? Get off your Golden Fleecing.
I will rub the window down until the pilot tells us
to put our chairs in position, ready to fly
into that sunset of remembrance's milk.

Amy King sent the Star Trek transporter beam,
the one from Next Gen, as my body turned to pure
energy, dematerialized to resurface far away from
Topeka, Kansas, so I could watch the Old World from
the viewscreen, Topeka at workin its Patriarchal
archways, sitting-pretty businesses protected by
moat, even along the Kaw, that river where a boatman
gives rides for two coins. My Oakland Neighborhood
accent gives me chords for survival, my mouth a gesture
of sincerity to any man I meet. These Christian-
American promises left this place, so a park remains
growing arteries, vines, disappears from the map.
It is Topeka Boulevard and Thirty-Seventh Street, just
in case you don't know speeding through the shortcut
on your way to a saccharine disco. *Language speaks
our very tender selves,* Amy comforts. I will birth
more swingsets, bushes, trees, anything I can
as I appear in silhouette, yes, I'm a man, too, but
can also make ships, call out to the stars, chart
a terrific smile, for real. Yes, I tremble, dissect
myself, because I ignored those chalk marks
for the women I knew who try and tried. Karate
won't help me now, nor help me get to know
anyone new. I'm looking for my jaw to move,
to speak mother-enveloping coos. These baby thumbs
learn to pry open the past, worn in a sling
instinctually close. I need a little oxygen
for my revolving sky.

Give me back this day my daily
cardinals, and forgive the sky
for its width. My gloves need
to come off if I count
one left hand, an eager minnow.
To write, I mean, is to throw off
the husk and Barbie pasts. You Kens
in your speedboats, I salute you
with my middle-finger bells.
If you can't hear them, let me turn them up,
the worst joke, you. I can't get past
these lungs full of breathing in Patriarchy.
I came to relax, and this room
just got stewing. The Devil don't wear
any tuxedo, but a fisherman's hat.
If Jesus wrote anything down,
it sure didn't survive you all. Now is the time
for piano, hymns to close with, effigy
of grass, bones, catfish, burning
in remembrance of women.

Do you sense me as your son
by your hospital bed, or is it
really me here, again? No.
I am in this light coming through
the television show of your pulse
in syndication. The nurses ask again
what relation I am to you, my mother's
partner. I'm asking again, what
beeping is that an alert for this time?
IV, feeding tube, or some other
thought I lost as, of course,
it is winter in Topeka.
You are my other mother.
My brain full of snow birds, this
January which should be for beginnings.
Is it time for you, the heartbreak
soldiers hold in their helmets?
Are we still on speaking terms
of atriums, aorta, rooms
I can't imagine but feel in
the ribs as a balloon? I can
imagine you pulling through,
arms of snow plows clearing
way for cardinals to return,
for me to hang up my frontier
to carry lanterns.

A Short History of Topeka

I'm in love with you, City, who doesn't know me
from the pages of any book I carry. I have to love
through the ink documenting any of my relatives, salt,
remaining cotton mills. Those men would gouge the eyes
of any shoulder shouldering in, drank in nectar
at the barstool, built their own homes and trees
just to watch the cherry blossoms blossom, with a month
later for the picking. With wine for your guitar playing,
we'll soon get the full story of night. Throw another
hammer so the railroad continues, so that mother
can call out again from fifty years ago looking for her son.
This is my fright, you know, as far as my boys are
concerned. Living here in the rich uncurled soil,
but surrounded by so many men with beer can meters,
time expiring, rifles loaded. Can that mother
call them in, too? Can we remember the kiss
you left, Topeka? There was a time something yoked,
they called it Revival, where that shadow now is.
Read her lips. See what she has to say.

You have quite a Friday night ahead of you
I might say to myself or to you, so
can you prove which you I am referring to?
This could be then or now, so let's call it
gone, fatal. Okay, okay, things are better,
whether this is Paris I am writing from, or Houston,
or Topeka, yes, it is here where these places
go missing. Then there is you. I am Great
Plains, faced East, back to the mountains.
That year of wishes, spooning the sun, living
off calzones, tacos, pinball, comic books,
bruises made by lightning, carrying on
with your lists, my lists. Yes, nails and teeth continue,
keeping optimistic despite your funeral. Though which
you can be proven? Which you smuggles
beer out of any place 'round here, toasts
highways, because once Topeka rises
again, reconnects with Los Angeles, New
York City, and Moscow, you, yes, you
as you, and I will stand
at John Curry Stewart's door, armed
with paintbrushes, ready to revive
the John Brown we need as we knock.

Kansas is in the middle, Topeka even more, so
this must be the saviour-city of ending struggle.
Okay, even I felt the segregation
through my hot-pants drive yesterday
in that neighborhood where the school still stands
for something to some visitor of the city's
limits. I hid from the devil
of our gangster government, when
we should send him and his lackeys
straight to the termites. I digress, those eyes
peer down in Orwellian style. Seas appear
here, and so does she, that teacher
from fifth grade who didn't know better
brains in the unbleached room,
so she transferred. Baseball economics
ruined our elbows and knees,
so I became friends with him
only, rock n' roll pariahs eating pizza
in the corner of the Great State of Kansas.
I gyrated my hips, he wailed on invisible stairs.
The moon came over us, just as it does
to those children of children still setting fires
in planned lines. Gets the cattle to move.

In some beer-filled afternoon
you will work to find me rising
as the short History of Topeka.
I'll recommend you pan gold
outside the dime store, to reclaim
what Kansas takes now
out of our souls. Did he really
mean that? Yes, I did
grow up with deprived Easters,
creatures snatching skins
in my labyrinth-patterned town.
Bread is made out of unswept land,
folds under four walls, which is why
hunger waits nude, fearful
of that wooden horse y'all carted in
when you spoke of thunder, oxygen,
a good place to plant potatoes, a sky
that blossoms forever, which even I
can't touch.

Even Topeka has the pleasure of lawn and trees
outside of the mall's obvious entrances, a carefree
winking after paid-off early retirements
help corporations in their syrupy blurs. Accept
that speed walking which hammers gerunds
into our language, promising the assertive
round of elegies. How does the need to claim
on your right feel to Kansas politics, the words
you use, your cushioned lips, those kisses
you tell? Do I need to mention Sam
in the midst of this ruin built decades ago?
Let the sun come through the dome window,
let the doves of love fly above that window,
let the window resign to the floor, let hammers
be heard, unseen, for comfort to our particles.

Visitors get entertained by the ghost
waitress raised on fried shrimp, handing out
peppermints to travelers of the Oregon Trail.
She escaped tornadoes by diving down
into the Kaw in her knickers, away
from the thick throats of men. Cross over
the front portal of the replica cabin
for cosmopolitan consumption, these stories
in chagrin when poverty strikes. If we are
the ninety-nine percent, this industry
withstands anything. Dime store still standing.
Indigenous nomenclatures still spoken.
Remote zones find us loose on American soil.
Mother of Topeka, keep a candle burning.
The takeover comforts now, thinking in terms
of merger in the way crossing the frontier west
is only a long walk. That pay phone don't work.
Take it from the lilacs, her voice as smooth
as inner thigh, the rotary machines were invented
just for us. These TV days spin frozen martinis,
lotto numbers, nights where you see a naked woman
swimming for all of our lives to shore.

I love the earth, really, and Carrie, my boys, the sky.
The list could go on. I won't. These stones
make death so obvious. This cemetery is old, no vacancy,
sufferers. Am I china plates and some bull is here
to stomp me? How apropos, that doves
fly here. Did Topeka's rotator cuff get torn, so
housing and business development flourished?
A cardinal says, hey. There's no point in silver
screens, murders, going AWOL in Kansas.
My sister and I have been fatherless many times,
motherless a few. I'm sobbing, you S-O-B! My fingers
twine my gray hairs, this pear is the planet, these seeds
do no good inert. I wish I had something good, City, today
to say in your stadium-shaped hole-in-one.

Wine, hide me now
inside dropped names
where the populace races
by without noticing
my bleeding skull, submerged
crown. I was king of yawns,
showing mercy along
this path of discovery,
but that was then, gin.
Today is a breeze
that hits my spine, shadows
of skin Topeka shed.
So these people do good
as long as they are happy,
the reason for the shiny streetlights,
reconstructed street as a place
inside? We want to be welcomed,
is this my motivation? How long
will this happy process last?
When will the goon show his lips,
ruin the permission? I will forgive
every one of those men
if music's mistress grounds
tonight in words. Break this divider
that runs the street, break the gaze.
Swim with me in the strawberries.
Revel in the dance that ignores
Guantanamo.

From the highest point overlooking the city's wonder,
apology stretched underneath the soil, a moth aching to
be set free. I sketch my profile on the monument,
that water tank marker marking shadows, demons set
free out of mouths. Let's get real. The graffiti warned us
about weight, about toes in the soil. I come up here to get
away from the hold Topeka thrusts, as if this place is
separate, apart like the thumb. Sure, drought followed
that tornado, you know the one if you're from here.
If you're from here, there will be a heaven, I'm sure.
There will be weeping.

To Photo the Future

Do I thumb through the right avalanche
that brings me circa whatever,
or turn the handle mistakenly
because of the wine I drink
at Flying Monkey, because
across the street Brian continues
playing that pinball game
while I read comic books, waiting
for one of my mothers to come
to pick me up? How can I already
be chained to each stupid day
back then, pulling apart
my mind's clothing? With thirst,
I need water to break my dehydration
of 1984, 1991, and 2004, at least
I think those years marked
by dandelions, my rolling
across the grass. I sit in corners
here, come find me
in a ball flipped by flippers.

Those dandelion seeds fall
out of my hands' skin, scatter
as I shout to my boys
not to touch them. How can I hide
dung, bells ringing, mission
drums, crucifixions? Carrie asks
about a place outside of this
country. Even rabbits
can't make it across this boundary
I wear in silence, shoulders
sloped, my coat's armor
shields out wind, rain, beast,
you, and this includes
me. What is my coin
of the realm doing
down the well?

An arm from that white rabbit
reaching up to take my
numbered memories? Days
trees get knocked down
along with abandoned buildings
to make way for new apartments,
commas, ellipses, waiting
to see death? I get up, shake
off my face, bury
costumes, drink wine, stagger
past houses, scream my policecar
siren and climb
up its vibrations. How could I
imagine never seeing you all again,
ghosts? I die
again, a drunk mummy
staggering to search for a new
tucking behind night. Romans
did this, so why can't the USA?

Quick, prevent the obedience
of kites, but pulling out scissors
is impossible. I get stuck here
yanking my cascading trigger
that keeps me here. Hand me
the letterpress of my birth, so I can
crank out caring. What happens
to the puppets is beyond me
or you, film projectionist. My
cinema treasures these films, fighting
off Nazis, evil wizards, psychokillers
I went to middle school with. He accused
me of talking about him behind
his back, but this chatter
is mine, all mine.

Even a baby crawls into the gutter
by mistake, so any fake
appearance bounces me somewhere
new, safe. Safety. Here's a turn, where
I confuse the fire in the window
for a change in infinity, or seek
contact where contracts are drawn
to take care of one, meaning me
wiped out, gone. It's awful how little
a bully's effort makes prisons
by mimicking plaster and bars
while no one cares about schoolyard
prophecies. Get me a rug to fly out
of this religion of ornate whips
and ordained paraphernaliacs. Who said
a scar or two couldn't help one
to photo the future?

People, hold on tight
to your souls, as natural history
comes sliding in with spoons.
Iraq? Which one, and at what circa
do you want me to respond in?
You know the army trucks never stop
for anything, even roses
or ghosts, and my friends
didn't have to go over to not be.
Climate is moving over
my hands and I can't stop this decay
myself, you lockjawed earth.
Our species is about to move
on, out the door, so what does it matter
if Topeka's lattice is overrun
by Sam? And so it goes, you
are right to put trust in the State
Capitol, right to allow them to vote
against GMO and rBGH labelling, right.
I believe the children are our future,
sang her, from a dream world
she did not find, but she is far away
from the Real, like us.

My mothers have had to put up
with the numbers, eating antibiotic
chicken, facing time, pushed out
by the lottery the town crier created.
But I like whomever, give everyone
a chance with my smile, nod, even
crackers in my neighborhood.
Still, binocular hallucinations show us
public theatres of, call it attacks
in the name of, pawns of some plan
some hater made based on the particles
of Patriarchy, or call it fear, Topeka.

But my doorbell rings, and somewhere
in the tall grass prairie is a vibraphone,
an abandoned nuclear missile silo converted
into a home, bruises bare, old world
cakes and pastries, kicks to a deserving
groin, frankincense waiting to be of value
again. Sam and his lackeys
are not defunct. To point and show
is a poet's burden, to write proof
underneath coffee mugs with grounds
at the bottom, channeling the voices
of all the drivers passing by and cardinals,
wearing skins of imagined animals
as they and we are at risk of extinction.
We are made criminals
for what we sunlight, but the barbed wire
pricks just a little, their factories
easy to see through. We wave the flag
for the workers, for the world.
But then the avalanche comes to keep us
stuck, all covered around us, so
start digging!

Any newborn's alphabet
is made of spike, sword, and gun
shapes. Zombies want us
to conceal and carry their words
in public spaces, books to attack
families, free speech held with baby gates
while grammar is checked, checked again.
I'm a walking paralysis, appear dead
but I'm liminal, within both worlds,
as the room's walls close in.

Many imitators and false heroes, but prairie
lightning frightens us back to the fist
which needs blocked by an arm
holding the writing hand. I place
kisses upon my spouse's feet
out of a means of caress, of need
to taste. There is a cover-up the news
places, about dinner, about shapes
factories make. After hours
while our sons sleep, we will talk
in Van Gogh tropes, a code
of horses and cleansing, arching
through until morning, will follow the curve
with our hands. Some man
forgets his rage, some chain
gets broken inside a hand
holding another.

Meanwhile, some
capitol-M Man finishes piling up
manure, plants his plans, essays
of [Man]ifestos, ready to eat
the worm at the bottom and become
King. Drones from phone calls
come to build a cell. Christmas
trees found hidden in the back
to raise their revolution, while
Sentinels seek out mutants. The New
Topeka Order breaks bread into crumbs,
while people question if eating each other
is viable in this limited-resource town.
When did our doorbell get broken?
Am I sounding too academic, snooty,
alphabetic in my delivery
as lessons keep retracting my
next thing to say, which is without
gardens or thought? No coincidence
we planted early, zucchini, tomatoes,
squash, and pumpkins so we will be set
after cruel summer, our tongues
replenished from the reverse osmosis
water we buy at Natural Grocer's
because the city puts something in
water, needs removed like toads
who crave attention. Kill other's
family values? My mothers'? How about
these children, yes, me and my sister,
who ended up all right?
Go see the movie already!

Hello, cardinals. Hello, winged
motions passing through needle eyes.
Love is the scalpel that does the trick
on tumors, on piecing together collages
for chapbook covers. Additional approaches
for the planet: I got God's ass covered,
my spine is a fine antennae for picking up
frequencies, let gay and lesbian couples
get married in their churches, your
courthouses, or wherever. These little things
connect through molecules, subatomic super
powers absorbed through the background.
This person or that might feel inconvenienced,
mass pulling down on her or him.
Even if you were born a boy, don't mean
I can't admire you as a brave woman.
Ten thousand objects, Lao Tsu told me,
jump into the wishing box, but my oldest son
shouts out his wish for, *Books!* Find
your earth's waist, cinch, and sew. I'm ready
for your help.

I want to make you safe,
Amy King told me once, not just me, but any you
who read it in her poem, read that poem
by the same title, read the book's title, enough
I needed no other need that day
to carry on in Topeka. God is out there,
out of minds, our minds collective
throughout space and time zones.
Sometimes these words get borrowed
but how else can I write? Any other time
I'm reading other words as jesters
jump through my spinal cord, make
my knuckle bones seize and thrust out,
but that's really not me. When did this anger
begin, God? I feel it through any civic ear,
stereos spreading carbon monoxide,
with my mouth down to the flowers, hoping
my breath out creates another breath in in
the cycle. This is only Topeka, though,
so hang on to my rib cage. Play the harp,
wind. Boys, please reattach
in our attachment parenting, as the wind
plays a song about holding onto love.

Dennis Etzel Jr. Dennis Etzel Jr. lives with Carrie and the boys in Topeka, Kansas where he teaches English at Washburn University. He has an MFA from The University of Kansas, and an MA and Graduate Certificate in Women and Gender Studies from Kansas State University. He has two chapbooks, *The Sum of Two Mothers* (ELJ Publications 2013) and *My Graphic Novel* (Kattywompus Press 2015). His first poetic memoir *My Secret Wars of 1984* (BlazeVOX 2015) was selected by The Kansas City Star as a Best Poetry Book of 2015. *Fast-Food Sonnets* (Coal City Review Press 2016) is a 2017 Kansas Notables Book selected by the State of Kansas Library. In addition to *My Grunge of 1991's* publishing in 2017, *This Removed Utopia* (Spartan Press 2017) was pub lished as part of the Kaw Valley Poetry Series. He is a TALK Scholar for the Kansas Humanities Council and leads poetry workshops in various Kansas spaces. Please feel free to connect with him at dennisetzeljr.com.

www.ingramcontent.com/pod-product-compliance
Lightning Source LLC
Chambersburg PA
CBHW021451080526
44588CB00009B/797